C O N T E N T S

Favorite
Find
32

Country
Rose
35

As Time
Goes By
43

Midnight Garden
Desk
39

Midnight Garden
Chair
42

INTRODUCTION

If you're a decorative artist, you already know the wonderful feeling of accomplishment that comes from transforming an everyday object into a beautiful accent piece for your home. Every time you glance at a finished project, or accept another visitor's compliment, the feeling comes over you again. It's the satisfaction of knowing, "I did it myself!"

Hand-painted furniture especially seems to inspire admiration. A coat of paint topped with a decorative design can turn a cast-off table or unfinished desk into a beautiful, one-of-a-kind heirloom.

Furniture decorating is a fun and creative outlet, but it's very practical, too. With a bit of effort, you can transform an inexpensive flea-market find, or create a lovely grouping from mismatched pieces that might not normally go together.

If you're a beginner, don't worry; we've included simple brushstrokes with illustrated instructions that, with a little practice, will allow you to paint any of the projects in this book.

These projects have all been chosen with beginning and intermediate painters in mind. Uncomplicated patterns and step-by-step instructions follow the pages of colorful photographs featuring lovely hand-finished furniture and accessories.

We've tried to include patterns and designs that can be used in many different ways so that you can adapt them to the particular furniture pieces that you may find.

Enjoy this book. I hope you'll be inspired to create your own conversation pieces to display in your home.

GENERAL INSTRUCTIONS

I always tell my beginning students to practice their strokes on paper before they start painting a piece. This familiarizes them with the brushes, the paint, and techniques such as side loading and washing. Once you're comfortable with the strokes, you're ready to begin.

Follow the instructions for your design and the color recommendations listed. Keep cotton swabs handy for correcting any mistakes.

Transferring the design

Use tracing paper and a Sharpie permanent marker to trace patterns. Lay the tracing paper over the pattern and trace it carefully with the marker. Then place the tracing paper over a piece of graphite paper (white or gray) graphite-side down on the object you'll be painting and tape lightly to secure. Go over your traced pattern with a stylus, tracing over the lines. Use light pressure so your lines won't be too dark and hard to paint over. Check your lines as you're tracing and make any adjustments.

Caring for brushes

When you purchase a new brush, clean it in water to remove any sizing. After using brushes, always clean them with a brush cleaner. Rinse with water and dry the brush on a paper towel, then reshape the bristles. Never let paint dry in the brush and never let brushes soak in water.

Mixing colors

In this book, when instructed to mix paints, the proportion is 1:1 unless otherwise stated. When proportions of paint are different, it will be indicated, such as 2:1, which means two parts of the first color and one part of the next. If paint is to be double-loaded, the colors will be listed as, "Double load with Sonoma Wine and Sachet Pink."

Setting up a wet palette

I use a thin plastic pencil box (available from stationery stores) lined with a piece of chamois cloth cut to fit. Then I cut a piece of deli wrap to fit and lay this over the top. Deli wrap can be found in grocery supply stores. The chamois holds a great deal of water and prevents the paint from drying out but doesn't allow moisture to dilute your paint.

Refinishing painted furniture

If you have an old piece of furniture that's painted, you'll need to strip (or remove) the paint. This is done with the help of paint stripper (available from paint or hardware stores). Follow the directions on the can very carefully.

Preparing furniture before painting

Sand the piece thoroughly using fine grit sanding disks. Remove the dust with either a tack cloth or a dampened cloth. Apply a wood sealer to seal any pores and to make the paint adhere smoothly.

Wet sanding

This method of sanding uses water on the sanding disk, which acts as a lubricant and makes for a smoother piece with less dust.

Basecoating

This means applying a smooth coat of paint over your surface. This will be the background of your design. For large pieces, use a foam brush or roller. For smaller pieces, use a wash brush.

Varnish

Two to three coats of exterior/interior varnish protects your beautifully painted piece of furniture. Sand between coats. You may select a matte, semi-gloss or high-gloss varnish.

⅝-inch flat shader

no. 18 flat shader

no. 16 flat shader

no. 14 flat shader

no.12 flat shader

filbert

no. 8 flat shader

no. 6 flat shader

no. 4 flat shader

no. 2 flat shader

no. 6 round

no. 4 liner

no. 2 liner

no. 1 liner

no. 0 liner

½-inch angle shader

no. 12 wave

no. 8 wave

no. 4 wave

½-inch angle wave

¼-inch angle wave

scruffy brush

JAN'S SUPPLY LIST

Brushes

I use the Black Gold line of brushes from Dynasty. You may wish to narrow down this list to an assortment of brushes you're most comfortable with.

nos. 0, 1, 2, 4 liner (206L)
no. 6 round (206R)
nos. 2, 6, 8, 10, 12 filbert
nos. 4, 8, 12 wave (206WV)
¼-inch (6mm), ⅜-inch (10mm), ½-inch (12 mm)
   angle wave (206WVA)
½-inch (12mm) angle shader (206A)
nos. 2, 4, 6, 8, 12, 14, 16, 18 flat shader (206S)
½-inch (12mm), ⅝-inch (15mm) flat shader (206G)
Scruffy brush (any worn brush)

Paint

Delta Ceramcoat acrylics are my favorite paints. They have a wide variety of colors so mixing paints isn't as necessary. They also have a rich, creamy consistency and offer great coverage.

Palette Knife

I prefer a metal palette knife with an angled shaft, which makes moving paint puddles easier. It's also more durable than a plastic one.

Sanding Disks

For sanding wood pieces, I use a fine-grit sanding disk. They are more durable than sandpaper, they hold their shape and they make it easier to sand hard-to-reach areas. They also hold up very well for wet sanding.

Paint Mediums

I like Delta Color Float for blending, shading and linework. For extending the drying time of paint, I use Delta Gel Blending Medium. Follow the manufacturer's instructions for using them.

Brush Basin

A brush basin is filled with water for cleaning brushes. Most have three compartments, one for swishing off the excess paint, one with a grid for vibrating the paint off the ferrule, and the third for storing clean water in order to do side loading.

Palette Paper

I prefer gray palette paper, which is available in tear-off pads. I keep a piece next to my wet palette for mixing paint and to stroke paint-loaded brushes.

Wet Palette

A wet palette keeps your paint moist while painting. (See General Instructions for Setting up a Wet Palette.) Cover your wet palette when you're finished painting and your paints will still be fresh the next day.

Stylus

A stylus is used to transfer your pattern from the tracing paper to your surface. A stylus has two points, one on each end. The stylus can also be dipped in paint and used to create dots.

Eraser

I use a Factis extra soft white eraser.

Cotton Swabs

To make corrections, I use a moistened cotton swab to lightly erase or remove mistakes. These can also be used for lifting excess paints or for making fluffy dots.

Marking Pen

For tracing patterns, use a Sharpie permanent marker with an ultra fine point. I like this pen because it doesn't smear and is permanent.

Other supplies

Delta All-Purpose Sealer
Delta Exterior/Interior brush-on varnish
Delta Faux Finish Glaze Base, clear
Delta Crackle Medium
Delta Brush Cleaner
Paper towels
Tracing paper
Scotch Magic tape
Sea sponge
Foam brushes
Pencil and sharpener
Rubbing alcohol

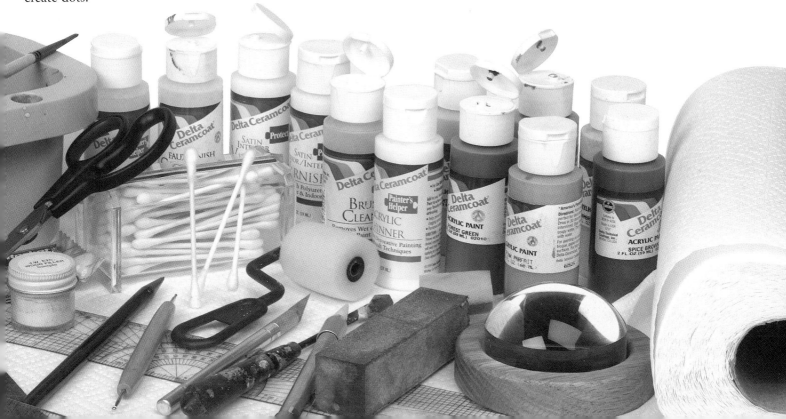

BRUSHSTROKES

Side Loading: 1. Clean a flat brush in water. Blot off excess water. Dip one side of brush into a fresh puddle of paint on the palette. Blend brush back and forth in the same spot at least five times to remove excess paint.

2. Paint will float gradually across the brush. Do not allow it to reach the other side. Remember that the wider the brush, the easier it is to float color.

Walking a Side Load: Load brush as in Side Loading step 1. Stroke brush as in side loading, moving brush slowly in the direction of the fade. Moving the brush too quickly will leave stripes (as shown at top).

Double Loading: Dip one side of the brush into one color of paint. Dip the other side into a second color. Stroke brush back and forth in the same spot until the two colors are blended in the center.

C-Stroke: Fully load a flat shader. Starting with the brush in a horizontal position, paint a "C." Do not let the brush twist between your fingers. The stroke should go from thin to thick to thin.

Open C-Stroke: 1. Start with your loaded brush at a 45° angle. Pull down to the left applying pressure to widen the stroke.

2. As you pull the brush, let it twist slowly back to a 45° angle.

Closed C-Stroke: With the loaded brush on a 45° angle, let the top of the brush twist from a 10:00 position to a 2:00 position, pushing up slightly at the 10:00 and pulling in slightly at the 2:00.

S-Stroke: 1. Using either a flat shader or a liner of your choice, load brush (flatten liner while loading). Start on the chisel at a 45° angle.

2. Then pull the brush to the left, then flatten to the right and lift to a chisel edge to the left. S-strokes should start and end at 45° angles.

Comma Strokes: 1. Load any size liner with paint, flattening the bristles while loading. The larger the liner brush, the larger the comma will be.

2. Press the brush down and pull toward you, lifting pressure as you pull. Comma strokes have a slight curve.

BRUSHSTROKES

Tear Drop Stroke: Using a fully loaded liner brush, press and pull toward you, twisting and lifting the brush as you pull.

Slip-Slap: Using a fully loaded flat shader, wipe excess paint on a paper towel. Make loose x's in a slip-slap motion to fill in area desired.

Stipple: Using a scruffy brush, dip brush into paint and pounce excess onto a paper towel. Gently tap desired area to get a light and lacy look.

Linework: Thin your paint to the consistency of ink. Hold the loaded liner brush with the tip of the brush grazing the surface. Slowly move the brush on the surface by moving your whole arm instead of your wrist.

Wave Stroke: Stroke in a leaf vein with a liner brush. With a fully loaded wave brush, stroke in toward the vein from the leaf point down, getting wider as you approach the base.

B-Stroke: With a loaded flat brush at a 45° angle, let brush twist from a 10:00 position to a 2:00 position, dipping in at the the center. Continue stroke to form a point.

Two-Stroke Leaf: Hold a fully loaded or double-loaded brush in a vertical position. Twist it between thumb and finger from 12:00 position to the 6:00 position, letting the brush flair out at approximately 4:00. Do the same in mirror image on the opposite side.

Half Circle: Hold brush in a vertical position. Twist the brush 180°, keeping the edge nearest to you stationary while moving the opposite edge around it. Do the same on the opposite side. Join them to make a full circle

One-Stroke Leaf: 1. Using a fully loaded or double-loaded brush, set the brush down, press and twist. Lift pressure on the brush gradually as you twist.

2. Twist the brush slightly and chisel-off (see page 10).

Jan's Hint:

You need to hold your brush firmly enough to control it, but don't use a "death grip." If you hold the brush too tightly, you'll end up with sore muscles in your hand.

9

BRUSHSTROKES

Consistent Dot: Dip the wooden end of your brush into a fresh puddle of paint and dot surface. In order for the dots to remain the same size, you must dip into the paint each time. The larger the brush, the larger the dot will be.

Graduating Dots: Dip the wooden end of your brush into a fresh puddle of paint and dot surface. Continue dotting without reloading the brush. Dots will get progressively smaller.

Set Downs: Using a fully loaded liner, set the bristles down creating an oval with the paint.

Chisel-off: Using a flat shader, fully, double-or side-loaded, start with the brush in a horizontal position. Pull brush toward you and let brush twist between your thumb and finger until the brush ends in a vertical position. Do not press, just guide the brush. When using a side-loaded brush, remember that the clean side of the brush must turn down.

Chisel Stroke: Fully load a flat shader. Using a side-to-side motion, pull the brush across the area on the chisel edge. Use this stroke to anchor an object.

Plaid: Use a fully loaded flat wave brush. With a light touch, stroke brush across area in one direction, then in the other direction.

Checks: Start by drawing light pencil lines with a straight edge or tape off edges. Use a flat shader brush and stroke consistent wide lines, touching the squares at the corners.

Jan's Hints: To load your brush, pour a puddle of paint onto your wet palette. Brush into the outer edge of the puddle with a damp brush. Applying pressure to keep the brush flattened, pull a small amount of paint out. Flip brush over and repeat, then stroke a few times on the palette paper. For blending, shading and linework, mix some Color Float medium into the paint on your palette.

Definition: "Pulling stroke" means making one continuous pulling motion with a brush.

ROCK-A-BYE ROSES

A rocking chair holds a special place in every heart, whether it reminds you of the place you first rocked your baby or the way grandmother used to rock by the fire. I found this dainty wooden rocker at a consignment store, already painted off-white. I was eager to enhance its charm with a few decorative touches!

I like to play up a chair's own assets, so I followed the cutout back design with delicate, swirling lines to emphasize its graceful shape. I chose this rose pattern to add to the antique feel of the piece.

Create your own beautiful little chair and you'll have a feminine accent for the bedroom, nursery or a shady porch!

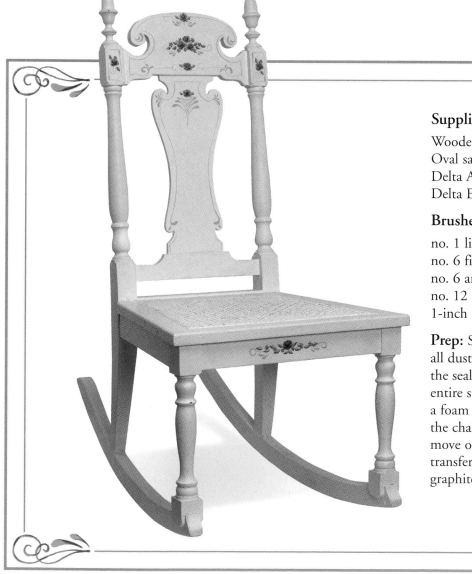

Supplies

Wooden rocking chair (new or vintage)
Oval sanding disk (fine grit)
Delta All-Purpose Sealer
Delta Exterior/Interior Varnish

Brushes

no. 1 liner
no. 6 filbert
no. 6 angle shader
no. 12 flat shader
1-inch (25mm) foam brush

Prep: Sand the piece well, and remove all dust with a dampened cloth. Apply the sealer using a foam brush. Basecoat entire surface with Seashell White and a foam brush. Tape the basic pattern to the chair so that it will be less apt to move on the curved surfaces. Then transfer the pattern to the chair using graphite paper.

Seashell White

Village Green

English Yew Green

Bahama Purple

Yellow

Sachet Pink

Sonoma Wine

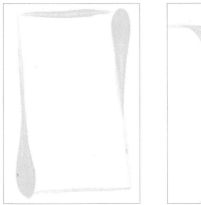  

1. Suggested life lines: Use a no. 1 liner brush and Village Green to create decorative lines (known as "life lines") following the curves and design of your particular chair. Use a variety of tear drop, linework and comma strokes (as shown above). All chairs will have a slightly different shape and design to them, so be creative with these lines.

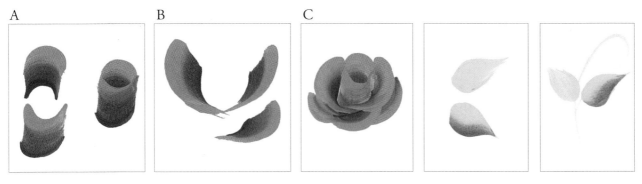

A   B   C

2. Roses: Double load a no. 6 angle brush with Sonoma Wine and Sachet Pink. Make two C-strokes, one on top of the other to form a tube (A).

Make flat comma strokes forming a 45° angle, pulling down to a chisel (B). Attach to each side of the tube, and add a stroke at the bottom (C).

3. Leaves: Use a no. 6 filbert and Village Green to stroke in some one-stroke accent leaves (see page 9) around the roses. Side load a no. 12 flat with English Yew Green to accent the bottom part of each leaf.

4. Blue flowers: Set down six small oval petals using a no. 1 liner and Bahama Purple. Dot Yellow in the center of each flower using the wooden end of the no. 1 liner.

5. After the piece is dry, finish with two to three coats of Delta Exterior/Interior Varnish.

13

TRAY CHIC

TRAY CHIC

This is another example of an object converted for a clever new purpose. I found a small table at a flea market—cute, but too small to be of much use. I decided to try attaching a new serving tray on top to form a larger, more useful table.

Of course, the first step was a decorative paint job for the plain tray! I used crumpled plastic wrap to achieve a textured look for the basecoat, then painted details in soft green to complement the painted table. The center features a simple grapevine wreath with tiny pink rosebuds.

The end result? A pretty side table that can hold a vase, photos or snacks in the bedroom or TV room. It's unique and useful too!

Supplies

Wooden tray
Small table
Delta All-Purpose Sealer
Delta Clear Faux Finish Glaze
  Base
½" (1.2cm) Scotch Magic tape
Plastic wrap
Delta Exterior/Interior Varnish
Wood glue

Brushes

nos. 1, 4 liners
nos. 6, 8, 10 filberts
⅜-inch (10mm) angle wave
no. 10 flat shader
½-inch (12mm) flat shader
1-inch (25mm) foam brush

Sandstone   Light Ivory   Lichen Grey   Spice Brown   Eucalyptus   Forest Green

Lisa Pink

Chambray Blue

Sunbright Yellow

1. Prep: Sand all rough edges of the tray, then seal the wood using the 1-inch (25 mm) foam brush and Delta All-Purpose Sealer. Let dry, then lightly sand the tray using the fine-grit sanding pad. Be sure to sand with the grain of the wood.

2. Basecoat: Base the entire piece using a 1-inch (25mm) foam brush and one coat of Sandstone. Let dry.

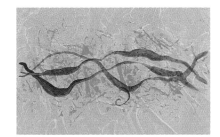

3. Faux finish: Have plastic wrap handy and a mixture of Light Ivory and Delta Faux Finish Glaze Base (1:2). Working in one area at a time, brush on the glaze mixture using a 1-inch (25mm) foam brush. While the mixture is wet, lay a piece of plastic wrap on top. The plastic should wrinkle. Create more wrinkles by using your fingers to crinkle the plastic. Lift off the plastic wrap and repeat on the next small section. Overlap edges to eliminate seams.

4. Wreath: Trace the design on the center of the tray. Dip a ball of crumpled plastic wrap into a mixture of Lichen Grey and glaze (1:1) and pounce off the excess on a paper towel. Pounce the glaze mixture around the wreath area.

5. Vines: Use a no. 1 liner and Spice Brown thinned to an inky consistency to create the vines that weave around the wreath. Use pressure on your brush for a wider vine and less pressure for a thinner vine.

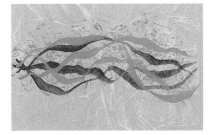

6. Do the same again, but with Eucalyptus, adding more vines to the wreath.

7. Small leaves: Use nos. 6 to 10 filberts (the size of the brush depends on the size of the leaves) and a mixture of Eucalyptus and glaze (1:1) to add one-stroke leaves (see page 9).

8. Large leaves: With the ⅜-inch (10mm) angle wave brush and Forest Green + glaze (1:1), stroke in leaves using the wave stroke (page 9).

9. Rosebuds: Double load the no. 10 flat with Light Ivory and

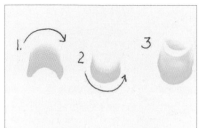

Lisa Pink to create rosebuds (above) using two C-strokes (see page 8).

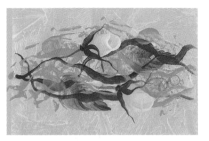

10. Stems & Calyxes: With the no. 1 liner and Forest Green, create stems on rosebuds.

Stroke in calyxes on rosebuds, as shown above.

11. Filler flowers: Using the no. 1 liner and Chambray Blue, put down three "set downs" (see page 10) all joined at one end. Dot the base of each blue flower with Sunbright Yellow using the wooden end of the no. 1 liner.

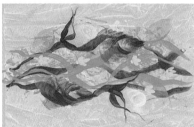

12. Rosebud centers: Dot the center opening of each rosebud using Sunbright Yellow and the wooden end of the no. 1 liner.

With the no. 4 liner and Eucalyptus, pull three comma strokes (see page 9) on each curve of the tray edge. Let dry.

Apply Delta Exterior/Interior Varnish. Using wood glue, attach the tray to the top of the small table.

13. Edges of tray: Tape off the edge of the tray using ½" (12mm) tape. Tape every other ½"(12mm) to form checks. Then basecoat the sections between the tape using a ½-inch (12mm) flat and Eucalyptus.

White

 Palomino Tan

 Raw Sienna

 Pink Parfait

Chambray Blue

 Leprechaun

WHIMSICAL WASHSTAND

There are countless ways to decorate this version of an old-style washstand. I've chosen a whimsical country design. It makes a charming accessory topped with a pitcher and bowl, potted plant, or…use your imagination!

For this design, I started with a base of Chambray Blue paint. The detailing includes simple plaid, floral, check and fancy flourishes. Note that some elements are repeated on the bowl and pitcher, and even the knob is painted to fit the scheme.

Many people use these stands in the master suite to hold rolled bath towels or add a pretty accent to the bedroom. Children can think of many creative ways to use this piece in their bedrooms, too!

Supplies

Washstand (Valhalla Wood)
Delta All-Purpose Sealer
Delta Exterior/Interior Varnish

Brushes

nos. 1, 4 liners
no. 12 wave
no. 8 flat shader
1-inch (25mm) foam brush

Prep: Sand any rough edges and surfaces. Remove dust using a dampened cloth. Apply Delta All-Purpose Sealer using a foam brush.

Basecoat the entire piece using a foam brush and Chambray Blue. Sand all edges of the washstand to give it an aged appearance.

21

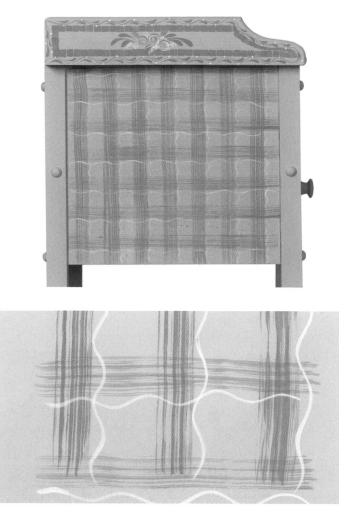

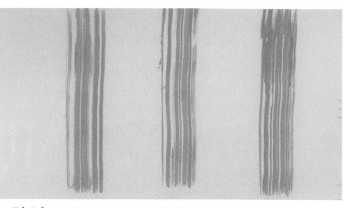

1. Plaid: You'll be painting all four sides and the round base area with the plaid design. Use a no. 12 wave and Pink Parfait to stroke vertical lines, leaving approximately 1" (25mm) between lines.

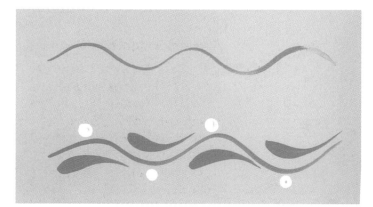

2. Then stroke horizontal lines with the same brush and Leprechaun. Use a no. 1 liner and White to pull a loose wavy line under each Leprechaun line and to the right of each Pink Parfait line.

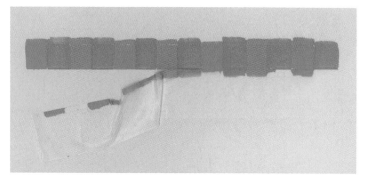

3. Checkerboard design: Tape off the top and bottom of the area to be painted with the checkerboard design. With a no. 8 flat, stroke alternating colors of Pink Parfait and Leprechaun for a line of checks. Remove tape when dry.

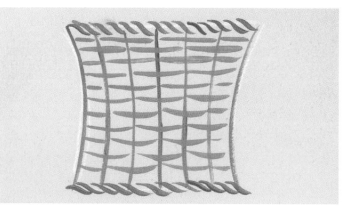

4. Wavy life lines: Pull a wavy life line around the edge of the area using a no. 1 liner and Leprechaun. With the no. 4 liner, pull comma strokes in between the waves of the life line. Use the wooden end of the no. 1 liner to place a dot of White next to the life lines as above.

5. Floral bouquet: Transfer the pattern using graphite paper.

Basket: With Raw Sienna and the no. 1 liner, pull vertical lines to form reeds of the basket. Use Palomino Tan and the no. 1 liner and place horizontal lines for basket weave. Using the same two colors, line S-strokes (see page 8) at the top and bottom of the basket.

6. Corkscrew flowers: Double load a no. 1 liner with Pink Parfait and White. Hold the brush straight up on point and line a corkscrew flower.

7. Leaves: Stroke in commas around the flowers using a no. 4 liner with Leprechaun.

8. Flowers: With White and the no. 4 liner, set down tiny daisy petals. Dot the centers of each with Palomino Tan using the wooden end of the no. 1 liner. Tap in little filler flowers using Pink Parfait and White on the wooden end of a no. 1 liner.

Apply two coats of Delta Exterior/Interior Varnish.

PITCHER & BOWL

Supplies

Ceramic pitcher and bowl
Krylon Matte Spray
Delta Exterior/Interior Varnish, gloss

Brushes

nos. 1, 4 liners
no. 8 flat shader

1. Prep: Spray the areas of the bowl and pitcher that you'll be painting with Krylon Matte Spray.

2. Checks: With the no. 8 flat and Pink Parfait and Leprechaun, create the alternating checks around the neck of the pitcher.

3. Life lines: Use the no. 1 liner to create life lines and the no. 4 liner to stroke commas next to the life lines. Use the wooden end of the no. 1 liner and Pink Parfait to dot along the life line.

4. Floral bouquet:

Use the no. 1 liner and Pink Parfait to create three corkscrew flowers. Stroke in commas around the flowers using a no. 4 liner with Leprechaun. Create tiny daisies using the no. 1 liner and Chambray Blue. Dot the center of the daisies and the corkscrew flowers with Palomino Tan and the wooden end of the no. 1 liner.

Using the tip of the no. 1 liner and Pink Parfait, dot little filler flowers. Finish with Delta Exterior/Interior Varnish.

FROM JAN'S GARDEN

Many furniture pieces can be used in new and creative ways, and decorative paint can play an exciting role in the transformation! This garage sale table is unique—a real find. It was originally a sewing machine cabinet, but the machine had been removed and replaced by a stainless steel basin. Painted ecru and aged with sandpaper, it was now an interesting convertible table with a sink.

The hardest work had already been done for me! With visions of a garden potting bench growing in my mind, I headed home to start decorating.

My design includes natural choices for a gardening theme—a watering can, terra-cotta pots, flowers and tools—with climbing ivy vines adding to the country-garden charm. Sitting out on the covered back porch, this is a wonderful conversation piece.

Think creatively as you look around. I'm sure you'll find many items that can be given new life with a little imagination and a decorative touch!

Terra Cotta

Drizzle Grey

Leprechaun

Georgia Clay

Bittersweet Orange

Bridgeport Grey

FROM JAN'S GARDEN

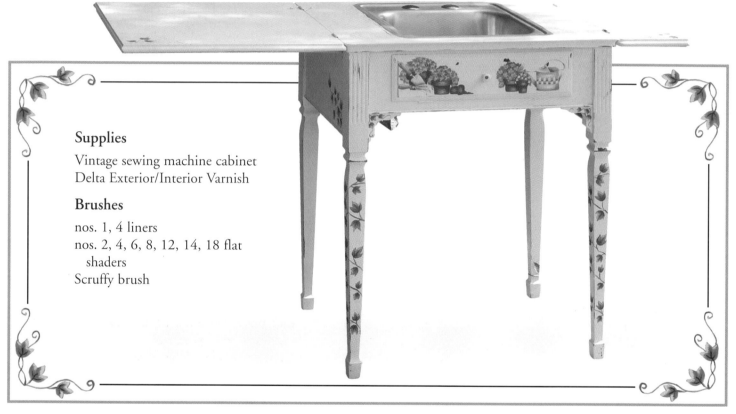

Supplies

Vintage sewing machine cabinet
Delta Exterior/Interior Varnish

Brushes

nos. 1, 4 liners
nos. 2, 4, 6, 8, 12, 14, 18 flat
  shaders
Scruffy brush

Prep: This piece was purchased already painted with a sink installed. If you find a sewing machine cabinet you'd like to convert, sand it completely, then basecoat it a solid color. For an aged appearance, sand all the edges.

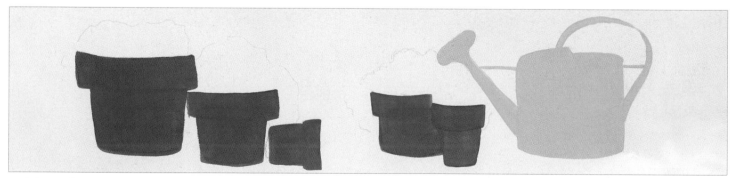

1. Trace design: Depending on your background color, use the appropriate color of graphite paper, then transfer the basic pattern to the cabinet. Transfer the trowel and hand fork after the pot has been completely painted.

2. Basecoat design: Using a no. 8 flat and Terra Cotta, basecoat the smaller pots. Use a no. 12 flat for the larger pots.

With no. 14 flat, basecoat the watering can with Drizzle Grey. Base the spout and handle using a no. 2 flat and Drizzle Grey.

Light Ivory

Brown Iron Oxide

Dark Jungle Green

Avocado

Tide Pool Blue

Village Green

Heritage Blue

Pink Quartz

Bahama Purple

Purple Smoke

White

Custard

Soft Grey

3. Shading and highlighting of pots: Re-transfer the pattern sections that need to be shaded. Use a no. 18 flat to shade the large pots with a side load of Georgia Clay, then with the 14 flat, shade the small pots. Shade both sides of all pots, fading toward the center of the pot. Shade under each rim, fading downward. The shades should all be nice and wide. Dip a scruffy brush into Bittersweet Orange and dry brush a highlight slightly off center on the right of each pot. For a second highlight use Bittersweet Orange + a touch of Light Ivory. Use Brown Iron Oxide to add a darker shade, going over the Georgia Clay.

4. Shading and highlighting of watering can: Side load the no. 14 flat with Bridgeport Grey and shade (as above). Shade the bottom of the can, but leave a small edge of the basecoat color to create the bottom rim. Paint a C-stroke (see page 9) in the center of the spout. Using a no. 12 flat and Soft Grey, stroke in a band of color across the center of the watering can. Using a no. 14 flat and a side load of Soft Grey, highlight the top of the spout, the left side of the top, and the handle where it attaches to the top. With a scruffy brush and Soft Grey, dry brush highlights above and below the band, on the handle, and on the center of each brace. Use a no. 14 flat and a side load of Light Ivory to paint a second highlight over all previously painted highlights.

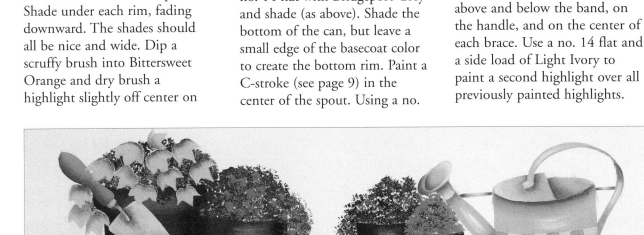

5. Tools: Transfer the pattern for the trowel and hand fork and the checks on the band of the watering can. Basecoat the tool handles with Tide Pool Blue using a no. 4 flat. Basecoat the metal parts with Soft Grey and a no. 6 flat (use a no. 4 liner to base the fork).

6. Greenery: Stipple greenery using a scruffy brush and Dark Jungle Green in the first and fourth pot, Avocado for the second pot, and Leprechaun for the fifth pot. Base ivy with Village Green and a no. 4 flat. Base the inside of the third pot using a no. 2 flat and Brown Iron Oxide, then stipple in the soil spilling out using the scruffy brush and Brown Iron Oxide.

7. Checks on watering can: Base every other block on the band of the watering can with a no. 6 flat and Tide Pool Blue. Shade near the bottom of each check with Heritage Blue.

8. Shade the fork and trowel with a no. 12 flat and a side load of Drizzle Grey. Shade the bottom of the handles using a no. 14 flat and a side load of Heritage Blue. Highlight the top of trowel with a no. 12 flat and a side load of White. Dry brush the fork with White using a scruffy brush.

Shade ivy leaves using a no. 12 flat and a side load of Dark Jungle Green. Highlight the tips of each leaf with a side load of Village Green. With a no. 1 liner, paint the veins in the ivy.

Stipple lightly here and there with a scruffy brush and Leprachaun over the Avocado foliage on the second pot.

Stroke in three-petal flowers using Pink Quartz and a no. 2 flat shader on the second pot. Dot the centers of the pink flowers with White using the tip of a stylus.

Double load a no. 4 flat with Bahama Purple and Purple Smoke and stroke in violets on the fourth pot. Dot small circles of Custard in centers.

Stroke in daisies on the fifth pot using a no. 1 liner and White. Dot the centers of the daisies using a stylus and Dark Jungle Green.

Dip a stylus in Heritage Blue and dot the holes in the spout of the watering can and on the handles of the tools. With a no. 1 liner and White, highlight around the holes on the handles.

9. Ivy leaves and vines: Trace the pattern for the ivy vine around the legs and on the sides of cabinet. Using a no. 1 liner and Leprechaun, paint the vines. Basecoat the leaves using a no. 8 flat and Leprechaun.

Shade with a side load of Dark Jungle Green at the back of each ivy leaf using a no. 14 flat.

With the no. 1 liner, paint the veins of the leaves. With a no. 14 flat and Village Green, side load highlights on the tips of each leaf.

When dry, finish with two to three coats of Delta Exterior/Interior Varnish.

FAVORITE FIND

If you're looking for a way to bring your decorative talents into a masculine domain, consider painting a handsome curio shelf. Purchased new and unfinished, this useful piece was painted black, and then decorated with an easy, two-stroke leaf design. Though it isn't specifically a masculine pattern, this leafy, natural look certainly couldn't be called feminine.

Because this design is so subtle, I used it generously on the piece. The leaves decorate the bottom drawer, top, molding and each shelf.

This curio would make a great gift for anyone, including your dad, husband or son. It could be used to display a small collection in an office or any room in the house. Where and with whomever it ends up, this handpainted shelf will be a constant reminder of you!

Light
Timberline
Green

Timberline
Green

English Yew
Green

Antique
Gold

Walnut

FAVORITE FIND

Supplies

Small Desktop Bookcase
Delta Instant Age Varnish
Delta Exterior/Interior Varnish

Brushes

no. 1 liner
nos. 8, 12 filberts

Prep: This bookcase was purchased already painted black. But if you find a similar one that is unfinished, you'll need to sand, seal, and basecoat it black. Sand all edges to give an aged appearance.

Transfer the pattern, adjusting it to fit your particular bookcase or shelf.

1. Using a no. 1 liner double loaded with Walnut and Antique Gold, pull vines. Paint two lines together to create vines for the corners of the shelves.

2. Leaves: Load the entire no. 8 filbert (or a no. 12 filbert, depending on the size of the leaf) with Timberline Green. Then side load one side of the brush in Light Timberline Green and the other side in English Yew Green.

3. Create one-stroke leaves (see page 9) on the vines. Paint a vein in each leaf using a no. 1 liner and English Yew Green.

Paint over the design using Delta Instant Age Varnish. Finish with two coats of Delta Exterior/Interior Varnish.

COUNTRY ROSE

This little footstool can be useful in many ways and it adds a colorful decorator touch to any space it occupies. Painted with a friend's color scheme in mind, this would make a wonderful surprise for Christmas or any gift occasion.

Unfinished wooden footstools can be found at your local craft or decorative painting store, along with the supplies needed to create your small work of art.

I used a crackle finish with green and cream to give this an aged look. The top and front areas show off a pretty floral design.

It isn't difficult to complete this project, and you'll be delighted with the results!

COUNTRY ROSE

Dusty
Mauve

Supplies

Wooden stool
Delta All-Purpose Sealer
Scotch Magic tape
Delta Crackle Medium
Sea sponge
Delta Glazing Medium

Brushes

nos. 1, 4 liners
no. 8 filbert
½-inch (12mm) angle shader
nos. 6, 12, 14, 16, 18 flats
¾-inch (19mm) wash brush
1-inch (25mm) foam brush

Prep: Sand the stool using a sanding disk. Seal using a foam brush and Delta sealer. Base the entire stool using Ivory and the 1-inch (25mm) foam brush.

1. Borders: Measure in 1" (25mm) all the way around the top of the stool. Tape off the inside section of the stool top. Paint this area with a ¾-inch (19mm) wash brush and Eucalyptus.

2. Base and crackle: Base the inside and outside surfaces of the legs using Eucalyptus and the ¾-inch (19mm) wash brush. Apply Crackle Medium according to the directions on the bottle. Allow to dry. Apply a coat of Ivory with either a sea sponge or a ¾-inch wash brush. Paint will crackle as it dries.

3. Side load Forest Green on a no. 18 flat and shade around the Ivory portion on the top of the stool (as shown in the picture above).

4. Lace: Using a no. 14 flat, side load White and scallop the lace on the Forest Green edge on the top of the stool using a C-stroke motion. Continue to side load with White and pull chisel-offs (see page 8) to form the base of each lace scallop. Allow to dry. Use a no. 1 liner and Eucalyptus to place a set down (see page 8) in each scallop of the lace.

Transfer the pattern to the top of the stool using gray graphite paper.

Ivory

Moss Green

Forest Green

White

Custard

Eucalyptus

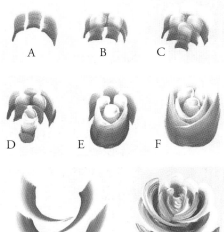

5. Background: Mix glazing medium with a touch of Forest Green. With a no. 16 flat, slip-slap (see page 9) over the basic pattern you've just traced. Let dry, then with a mix of glazing medium and a touch of Dusty Mauve, slip-slap again over the Forest Green area.

6. Leaves: Double load a no. 14 flat with Forest Green and Moss Green. With the Moss Green on the outside, stroke in large two-stroke leaves (see page 9). With a no. 1 liner and Eucalyptus, pull vines. Use a no. 1 liner and Forest Green to pull veins and stems of large leaves. Double load a no. 8 filbert with Forest Green and Moss Green and pull small one-stroke leaves on the vines.

7. Roses: Double load a ½-inch (12mm) angle brush with Dusty Mauve and White. Paint a C-stroke with two breaks (A). On top of this, paint a second C-stroke with one break (B). Then paint one C-stroke overlapping its bottom half (C).

Over this, use a single C-stroke to form a tube for the rose's center (D). Paint two large comma strokes, connecting the ends of the second C-stroke (E). Paint two more large comma strokes, connecting them to the ends of the first C-stroke (F).

Make flat comma strokes forming a 45° angle, pulling down to a chisel (G). Cover the bottom of the rose with these petals (H).

8. Five petal flowers: Double load a no. 6 flat with Dusty Mauve and White. Paint flowers using closed C-strokes (see page 8).

9. Stroke in commas on the vines with Dusty Mauve and a no. 4 liner. Use a no. 12 flat and Dusty Mauve to tint the sides of the large leaves.

With a no. 1 liner and Custard, paint comma strokes in the centers of the small flowers. Tap pollen in the centers of the roses using the tip of a no. 1 liner and Custard.

10. Filler flowers: Create graduated dots of White using the wooden end of the no. 1 liner (see picture at left).

Apply two coats of Delta Exterior/Interior Varnish.

MIDNIGHT GARDEN

Custard   Antique   Raw Sienna   Autumn   Pink   Coral
                 Gold   Brown   Frosting

DESK, CHAIR AND CLOCK

I found this desk and chair at a garage sale and was drawn by the matching, antique-style spindle legs. To emphasize the vintage feel of these reproductions, I painted them with a unique black base, and then chose deep, warm colors for the decorative touches. A subtle floral and leaf design was all that I needed to enhance the beauty of these pieces. With aging varnish and a little sandpaper, this duo was "worn" to perfection!

To create the feel of a coordinated grouping, I purchased a ready-to-paint clock to go with this set. The base is a contrasting cream color, shaded with the same golden tones found on the desk and chair. The center displays the floral pattern to match the other pieces.

This grouping could be placed in a large kitchen or entryway, or would be at home in a bedroom or den. I think it would make a great little writing or telephone station.

MIDNIGHT GARDEN DESK

Supplies

Vintage desk (found at a garage sale)
Delta All-Purpose Sealer
Delta Metallic 14K Gold paint
Delta Instant Age Varnish
Delta Exterior/Interior Varnish

Brushes

no. 1 liner
½-inch (12mm) angle shader
nos. 8, 10, 12, 14, 18 flat shaders
2-inch (50mm) foam brush
Scruffy brush

Prep: Sand, seal, then basecoat using Black and a 2-inch (50mm) foam brush. Allow to dry. Sand the edges of the desk for an aged appearance.

| Red Iron Oxide | Lemon Grass | Light Timberline Green | Timberline Green | English Yew Green | Black Green |

1. Gold corner decoration:

Use the wooden end of a no. 1 liner to place graduated dots of Metallic 14K Gold in each corner. Stroke in comma strokes on each side of the dots. Continue with a line all around the drawers. Follow these same instructions for the top of the desk.

Transfer the basic pattern to the front of the desk. Use the portion of the pattern that fits your particular piece.

2. Base leaves: Use a range of flat shaders from no. 8 to no. 14

(depending on the size of the leaf). Double load the brush with Timberline Green and Light Timberline Green and paint the large two-stroke leaves.

3. Base vines: With a no.1 liner and Timberline Green, line in the vines. Then flatten the no. 1 liner, double load it with Timberline Green and Light Timberline Green, and pull in strokes for the leaves of the vine.

4. Base flowers: Using a no. 8 flat and the B-stroke (see page 9), base the

small pink flowers with Coral.

With a no. 12 flat and Antique Gold, base in the yellow flowers at right using B-strokes.

Use circle-strokes (see page 9) with a no. 8 flat and Antique Gold for the yellow flower at left.

Base the rose and rosebud using Coral and a no. 14 flat.

Follow these instructions for the flowers and vines on the right side of desk front (not shown above).

5. Highlight and shade flowers:
For the small pink flowers, use a no. 8 flat with a side load of Pink Frosting to highlight the outside edges.

Use a side load of Custard on a no. 12 flat to highlight the edges of all of the yellow flowers. Then shade the flowers using a side load of Raw Sienna and a no. 14 flat. Shade a second time with a side load of Autumn Brown on a no. 14 flat.

6. Highlight and shade leaves:
Using a no. 18 flat and a side load of English Yew Green, shade all two-stroke leaves. Use a side load of Lemon Grass and no. 18 flat to highlight the tops of the leaves.

Shade the leaves a second time with a double load of English Yew Green and Black Green in the darkest areas.

7. Rose: Using a ½-inch (12mm) angle, side load the bowl and throat of the rose with Red Iron Oxide C-stroke.

Follow the same instructions for the right side of desk front (not shown above).

8. Flowers: For the three small pink flowers, use a no. 14 flat side loaded with Red Iron Oxide to shade the inside edges of each petal. Then use a no. 1 liner and Red Iron Oxide to pull lines out from the center of each petal. Use a no. 14 flat and Red Iron Oxide to shade where the flowers overlap.

Dip the wooden end of the no. 1 liner in Antique Gold and dot in the center of each flower.

Double load a scruffy brush with Red Iron Oxide and Coral to stipple the center of the yellow flower on the left.

Keep the Coral toward the top and the Red Iron Oxide toward the bottom, moving in a circle. Stipple in Pink Frosting highlights.

With Red Iron Oxide and a no. 1 liner, pull lines out from the centers of the two yellow roses on the right. With the scruffy brush double loaded with Red Iron Oxide and Coral, stipple smaller areas onto the yellow flowers on the right. Also stipple Pink Frosting highlights.

Then use a ½-inch (12mm) angle double loaded with Coral and Pink

Frosting to stroke in the rose and rosebud (see rose instruction page 37).

Use a no. 1 liner double loaded with Timberline Green and Lemon Grass to stroke in a calyx, and stem on the rosebud, and all other stems.

Allow to dry. For an antique appearance, apply a coat of Delta Instant Age Varnish over the top of the painting. Follow the instructions on the package.

If desired, you may add coats of Delta Exterior/Interior Varnish.

MIDNIGHT GARDEN CHAIR

Supplies
Chair
Same as for desk, see page 40

Brushes
Same as for desk, see page 40

Prep: Sand, seal, then basecoat chair using a foam brush and Black. Sand edges to give an aged appearance. Trace the pattern on the desired areas of your chair.

Follow the instructions for the desk (pages 41 and above) to paint the flowers. For the leaf vine of the seat, follow instructions on page 33 for "Favorite Find."

Apply a coat of Instant Age Varnish. When dry, add two coats of Delta Exterior/Interior Varnish.

Palomino
Tan

Burgundy
Rose

Light
Timberline
Green

Timberline
Green

Antique
Gold

Pink
Frosting

Ivory

AS TIME GOES BY

Supplies

Clock (Wizards of Wood)
Delta Instant Age Varnish
Delta Faux Finish Glaze
   Base, clear

Brushes

no. 1 liner
nos. 2, 12 filberts
½-inch (12mm) angle shader
nos. 12, 14 flat shaders
Scruffy brush

Prep: Mix the glaze with Palomino Tan (2:1). Slip-slap (see page 9) unevenly under the pattern area.

Transfer the pattern to the center of the clock face.

1. With a no. 1 liner and Palomino Tan, paint in the vines. Allow to dry, then use Light Timberline Green to create more vines.

Use a no. 2 filbert to stroke on the buds, alternating with the Palomino Tan and Light Timberline Green.

2. Double load a no. 12 filbert with Light Timberline Green and Timberline Green to create basic two-stroke leaves (see page 9).

Basecoat the wild roses on top with a no. 14 flat and Ivory.

Mix Burgundy Rose and Pink Frosting (1:1), and with a no. 14 flat, base the rose and the rosebud.

3. Side load a no. 14 flat with Antique Gold and stroke in the shading between petals and at the base of each petal on the two ivory wild roses. Stipple the centers of the wild roses with Timberline Green and a scruffy brush.

With a no. 14 flat side loaded with Burgundy Rose, paint a C-stroke in the bowl and throat of the pink rose.

4. Reinforce the shading on the wild roses with a side load of Burgundy Rose and a no. 14 flat. Then with a scruffy brush and Burgundy Rose, stipple the centers of the wild roses. Double load a ½-inch (12mm) angle with Burgundy Rose and Pink Frosting and stroke in the rose (see rose instructions, page 37). Shade the base of the bud with a side load of Burgundy Rose.

Paint the stem on the rosebud using a no. 1 liner and Timberline Green. Then, with the same brush and Timberline Green, paint the calyx of the bud (see page 18).

Apply a coat of Delta Instant Age Varnish.

Join pattern here

Enlarge 120%

1/2 of Desk Front Pattern

1/2 of Desk Front Pattern

Top of Chair

Bottom Front of Chair

Join pattern here

Join pattern here

46

PAINT CONVERSION CHART

Ceramcoat® by Delta	Americana™ by Decoart	Folk Art® by Plaid
Antique Gold 2002	Antique Gold	Yellow Ochre
Autumn Brown 2055	Light Cinnamon	Brown Sugar
Avocado 2006	Antique Green+Antique Gold 2:1	Olive Green+Teddy Bear Tan 1:1
Bahama Purple 2518	Wisteria	White+Periwinkle 3:1
Bittersweet Orange 2041	Tangerine+Cad Orange (T)*	Glazed Carrots
Black Green 2116	Black Green	Wrought Iron+Payne's Grey
Brown Iron Oxide 2023	Light Cinnamon+Dark Chocolate 4:1	Maple Syrup
Burgundy Rose 2123	Brandy Wine	Huckleberry
Chambray Blue 2514	White+French Grey Blue 5:1	Porcelain Blue+White 2:1
Coral 2044	Coral Rose	Salmon
Custard 2448	Taffy Cream	Lemonade
Dark Jungle Green 2420	Evergreen	Olive Green
Drizzle Grey 2452	Dove Grey+Grey Sky 4:1	Light Grey+Porcelain Blue 12:1
Dusty Mauve 2405	Cranberry Wine+Dioxazine Purple 3:1	Purple Passion
English Yew Green 2095	Plantation Pine+Avocado 4:1	Olive Green+Southern Pine 1:1
Eucalyptus 2569	Hauser Medium Green+Celery 1:1	Hauser Med Green+Bayberry+ Med Green 1:1:1
Forest Green 2010	Avocado+Evergreen 2:1	Old Ivy
Georgia Clay 2097	Burnt Orange	Terra Cotta+Autumn Leaves 1:1
Heritage Blue 2415	Uniform Blue+Charcoal Grey 5:1	Heartland Blue+Charcoal Grey 4:1
Ivory 2036	Sand	Taffy
Lemon Grass 2568	Limeade	Lime Yellow
Leprechaun 2422	Jade+Forest Green 3:1	Mystic Green
Lichen Grey 2118	Driftwood	Barn Wood
Light Ivory 2401	Light Buttermilk	Warm White
Lisa Pink 2084	Baby Pink+Spice Pink (T)*	White+Calico Red 4:1
Light Timberline Green 2531	Antique Green+Sand 1:1	White+Olive Green+Teddy Bear Tan 2:2:1
Moss Green 2570	Desert Sand+Jade 3:1	Basil Green+White 1:1
Palomino Tan 2108	Cool Neutral+Milk Chocolate 2:1	Teddy Bear Tan
Pink Frosting 2461	Hi-Lite Flash	Cotton Candy
Pink Parfait 2525	Boysenberry Pink+White 2:1	Pink
Pink Quartz 2474	White+Raspberry 3:1	Raspberry Sherbet+White 1:1
Purple Smoke 2548	Blue Violet+Violet Haze 3:1	Midnight+Lavender 3:1
Raw Sienna 2411	Raw Sienna	Yellow Light+Terra Cotta 2:1
Red Iron Oxide 2020	Red Iron Oxide	(no match)
Sachet Pink 2464	French Mauve	Berries 'N Cream
Sandstone 2402	Desert Sand	Clay Bisque
Seashell White 2541	White+Spice Pink (T)*	Rose White
Soft Grey 2515	White+Dove Grey+Grey Sky 4:4:1	Grey Mist+Dove Grey 4:1
Sonoma Wine 2446	Rookwood Red	Wild Rose
Spice Brown 2049	Milk Chocolate	Nutmeg
Sunbright Yellow 2064	White+Lemon Yellow 1:1	Yellow Lemon
Terra Cotta 2071	Terra Cotta+Burnt Orange 3:1	Glazed Carrots+English Mustard 2:1
Tide Pool Blue 2465	French Grey+White 2:1	Porcelain Blue
Timberline Green 2533	Plantation Pine+Pumpkin 5:1	Olive Green+Teddy Bear Tan 2:1
Village Green 2447	Jade Green+White 1:1	Poetry Green+White 1:1
Walnut 2024	Raw Umber	Raw Umber+Coffee Bean 3:1
White 2505	White	White
Yellow 2504	Primary Yellow	School Bus Yellow

*T - Touch of

SOURCES

Brushes
Black Gold by
Dynasty
70-02 72nd Pl.
Glendale, NY 11385
www.dynasty-brush.com

Paint, Mediums, Varnishes
Ceramcoat
Delta Technical Coatings
2550 Pellissier Pl.
Whittier, CA 90601
www.deltacrafts.com

Surfaces

Washstand by Valhalla Designs
343 Twin Pines Dr.
Glendale, OR 97442
(541) 832-2736

Clock by Wizards of Wood
(800) 237-6578

Most of the products featured in
this book may be ordered from:
The Painting Goose
28780 Old Town Front St.
Temecula, CA 92590
www.the paintinggoose.com

CREDITS

Produced by
Banar Designs, Inc.
P.O. Box 483
Fallbrook, CA 92088
banar@earthlink.net
www.banardesigns.com

Art Direction: Barbara Finwall
Editorial Direction: Nancy Javier
Photography: Stephen Whalen
Photo Styling: Barbara Finwall
Computer Graphics: Wade Rollins
and Chris Nelsen
Project Direction: Jerilyn Clements
Writing: Susan Borsch
Editing: Jerilyn Clements, Nancy
Javier, Victoria Dye
Pattern Illustrations and Project
Testing: Victoria Dye

MAKE YOUR HOME MORE BEAUTIFUL WITH DECORATIVE PAINTING!

These books and other fine North Light titles are available from your local art & craft retailer, bookstore, online supplier or by calling 1-800-448-0915.

Add beauty and elegance to every room in your home! Diane Trierweiler makes it easy with step-by-step instructions for giving old furniture a facelift and new furniture a personal touch. You'll learn how to paint everything from berries to butterflies on chests, chairs and more. Includes 12 complete projects with color charts and traceable patterns.

ISBN 1-58180-234-X, paperback, 128 pages, #32009-K

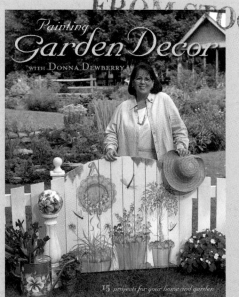

Transform your everyday outdoor furnishings into stunning, hand-painted garden accents. Acclaimed decorative painter Donna Dewberry shows you how to transform 15 deck, porch and patio pieces into truly lovely garden décor. Donna's easy-to-master brushwork techniques make each one fun and rewarding. No green thumb required!

ISBN 1-58180-144-0, paperback, 144 pages, #31889-K

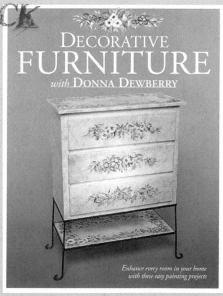

Donna Dewberry shows you how to master her legendary one-stroke technique for painting realistic flowers, fruits and other decorative motifs. Simple step-by-step instructions accompany each project. Guidelines for matching color combinations to existing room schemes enable you to customize every project to fit your décor!

ISBN 1-58180-016-9, paperback, 128 pages, #31662-K

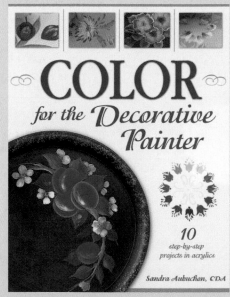

This guide makes using color simple. Best of all, it's as fun as it is instructional, featuring ten step-by-step projects that illustrate color principles in action. As you paint your favorite subjects, you'll learn how to make color work for you. No second-guessing, no regrets-just great-looking paintings and a whole lot of pleasure.

ISBN 1-58180-048-7, paperback, 128 pages, #31796